RIBA **ӝ**

Chartered Practice

LONDON
Unit 12 Printing House Yard
15 Hackney Road
London E2 7PR
+44 (0) 207 729 5035

ATHENS
Ploutarchou 30
106 76 Athens
+30 210 33 87 563

divercityarchitects.com
info@divercityarchitects.com

Welcome

Divercity Architects is an architecture and interior design studio with offices in London (RIBA Chartered Practice) and Athens. Our international portfolio includes hotels and restaurants, private residences, apartments and offices, student housing and cultural institutions. Our award-winning designs have been published worldwide.

Delight in surprise. Our name comes from our openness to a multitude of influences and our curiosity about contemporary urban living. We embrace the power of technical innovation to take architecture in new directions, both in terms of how we imagine space and use modern materials.

A sense of place. Our ideas are grounded in respect for local heritage and craftsmanship. Rigorous research allows us to develop strong design concepts that make sense in their particular physical and cultural context.

Every building tells a story. From Mykonos to St Moritz, the Argentine pampas to the Algarve, every project is a journey into new landscapes and lifestyles that inform and inspire our ideas. What threads our practice together is a narrative-driven approach to space that engages all the senses.

One size does not fit all. Never formulaic, our buildings are designed for people with a strong sense of identity and individuality. We don't impose a particular style on our clients. This collaborative attitude is reflected in the diversity of our work. We listen to your aspirations, reveal possibilities, and then develop the most effective blueprint to build your dream.

Beautifully designed, brilliantly executed. Project management matters as much to us as creative thinking. We get just as excited about building materials and budgets, as sketches and scale models. We make things simple for our clients, pulling all the elements together into a disciplined and clear process to see everything through from concept to construction.

Built to last. We define sustainability as environmentally sensitive architecture that can adapt to change. What matters most is how people will inhabit and interact with the buildings we create. This three-dimensional thinking translates into dynamic spaces that make an impact, but always serve a purpose.◀

Divercity Architects

One Athens

—▼—

One Athens is an exclusive residential development in a prime Athens location. The 26 apartments, duplexes, penthouses and townhouses come with five-star facilities, including a concierge, private gym with indoor pool, playroom and screening room, and a stunning roof garden with sweeping city views.

An icon of modern Greek architecture, the building was originally designed in 1957 as the headquarters of the visionary architect and urban planner Constantinos Doxiadis. The building had been abandoned for over 20 years when we were invited to revive its fortunes. Our challenge was twofold: the sensitive revival of a landmark imprinted on the city's collective memory, and the conversion of an office building into high-end residences.

Award

The European Union Prize for Contemporary Architecture, Mies van der Rohe Award
Nominated, 2015

Divercity Architects

Clockwise from above: Light and shadow are filtered through the textured surfaces of the facade.

The volumes are aligned with the sloping site and neighbouring apartments. Floor-to-ceiling windows maximise the views of pine-covered Mount Lycabettus.

The open-air atrium, an important feature of the original building, is designed to create a strong sense of community and place.

The original Doxiadis Building, designed in 1957. Image from the book *C. Doxiadis, Texts, Design Drawings, Settlements*.

Our approach was inspired by Doxiadis' theory of Ekistics: he believed urban architecture should create a sense of community through open, engaging buildings that can accommodate a variety of lifestyles. Doxiadis studied the history of human settlements, but embraced technological evolution to shape the cities of the future.

Maintaining the elegant simplicity of the structure, the new design is faithful to Doxiadis' legacy but forward-looking in its cutting-edge design. We preserved the original grid construction, but updated the modular facade with alternating panels of marble, translucent concrete, and glass to distinguish the open-plan interiors. The interplay of materials creates more versatile, private, and composite spaces, combining intimacy and transparency. The interiors have a dual aspect, bringing both the forest and cityscape into sharp relief, and reconnecting the building with its surroundings.

Set on a steep slope, four buildings of escalating height are set around a central courtyard, originally modelled on a Greek village square. In this spirit, the entire ground floor is dedicated to communal spaces, revolving around a marble-clad atrium. ◄

Clockwise from above: Herringbone wooden floors and exposed concrete ceilings pay homage to the 1960s 'golden age' of Athenian apartment buildings.

The soaring lobby creates the sensation of entering a five-star hotel.

Grey marble floors extend from the atrium to the indoor pool, creating a seamless flow accentuated by reflective glass.

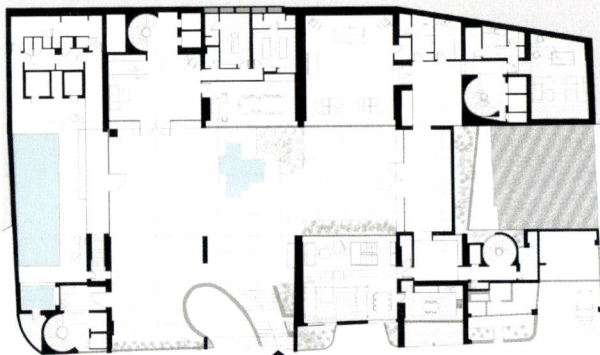

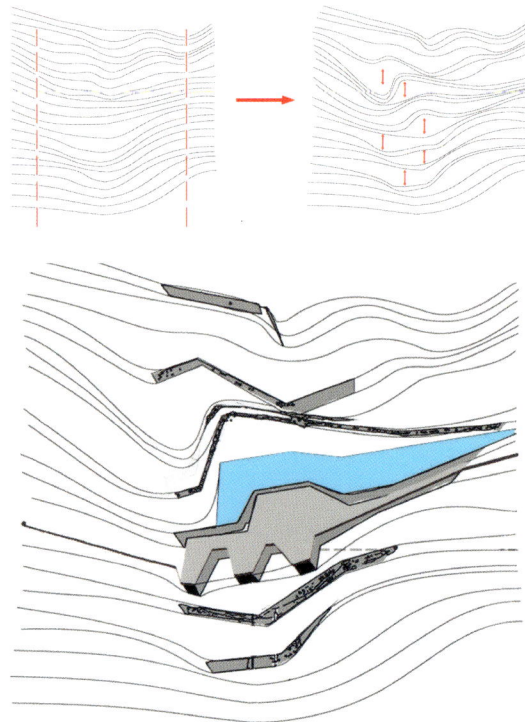

Grace Santorini

—▼—

Grace Santorini is a five-star hotel, suspended 300 metres above the island's volcanic caldera. Our iconic design, in collaboration with Mplusm, allows this extraordinary landscape to take centre stage.

Like the traditional island dwellings, *yposkafa*, rooms and suites are carved out of the cliff-face. Instead of typical rounded walls and domed roofs, we opted for sharper, more contemporary lines that protect residents from passers-by, while drawing the gaze towards the horizon. Inspired by the geological strata of Santorini's cliffs, the hotel slots into the landscape like a stack of stone ledges. The broken geometry of the boundaries reflects the jagged outline of Skaros, the ruins of a medieval citadel eye-level with the site.

Awards

World Architecture Festival Awards, Holiday and Hotels
Shortlisted, 2011
World Architecture News, Hotel of the Year
Shortlisted, 2011
The European Hotel Design Awards,
Shortlisted, 2010

The angular infinity pool echoes the paths
that zigzag across Santorini's rocky terrain.

Divercity Architects

Above: Cascading grey and white terraces and volcanic stone walls are imagined as a continuation of the landscape.

Divercity Architects

S antorini's hotel rooms are usually open-ended to face the view, leaving guests exposed to the elements and passers-by. We subverted this trend, placing a lattice of volcanic rocks in the windows to filter the sunlight, providing privacy and ventilation. The boulders also screen the plunge pools, their apertures offering tantalising glimpses of the unbroken horizon.

Pristine interiors in contrasting tones of volcanic black and Cycladic white, organic materials, and cubist forms all refer to Santorini's architectural trademarks, without slipping into cliché. We also designed the hotel's piece de resistance: a stand-alone villa with a private pool and spa. ◄

Above: In the restaurant, a dark feature wall that echoes the volcanic landscape is punctuated with lights that glow like lava.

Below: Black and white patterns on the floors mirror the irregular shapes of the volcanic rocks, the white outlines typical of traditional Cycladic paving stones.

Divercity Architects

Natural 'shutters' of exposed rocks cast dappled shadows and
cocoon guests from the fierce sun. This unusual feature echoes
a local building technique more commonly applied to retaining
walls, using minimal amounts of mortar.

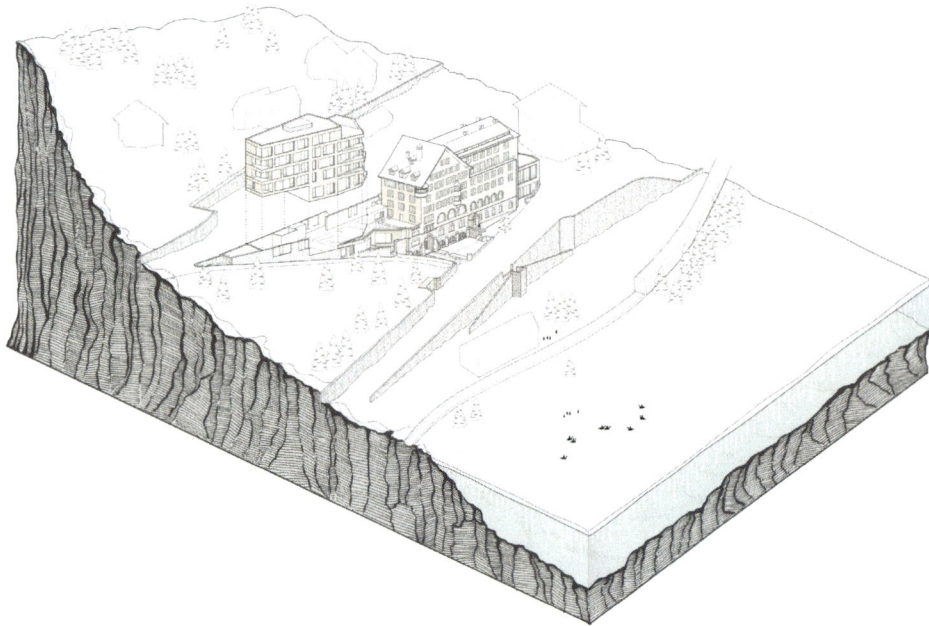

Grace St Moritz

— ▼ —

Built at the turn of the 20th century,
La Margna Hotel has been a local institution
in St. Moritz for generations. Its new owners,
Grace Hotels, wanted to rebrand the hotel
with an iconic renovation. Our challenge
was to refresh the original architecture, while
adding a modern extension for additional
rooms and a spa. As well as accommodating
strict building regulations and the constraints
of a sloping site, the brief called for flexible
hotel rooms that could be reconfigured
as long-stay apartments.

We came up with a design that connects
old and new, by extending the base
of the existing building. Set on a series
of terraces that follow the natural incline,
the unobtrusive extension is neatly integrated
into the landscape. Inspired by natural
fissures in the icy slopes, the building is
broken into multiple levels oriented towards
the views. Deliberately discreet, the new wing
does not upstage the traditional architecture
and stunning Alpine setting.

A subtle update on its gabled predecessor,
the new wing fits snugly alongside the original
Art Nouveau hotel.

Picture windows and adaptable, open-plan interiors create a sense of light and space; a welcome antidote to Switzerland's dark, wood-clad chalets and opulent grand palaces. This is a hotel that feels like home. ◀

Clockwise from above: Cosy but uncluttered, interiors are dressed in warm timber and soft textiles. Lighter materials near the windows turn attention towards the wide-open spaces outside.

A modern take on Alpine style, bedrooms are brighter and lighter than typical chalets.

The clever layout allows apartments to be transformed into separate suites, simply by opening or closing multiple entrances in the corridors.

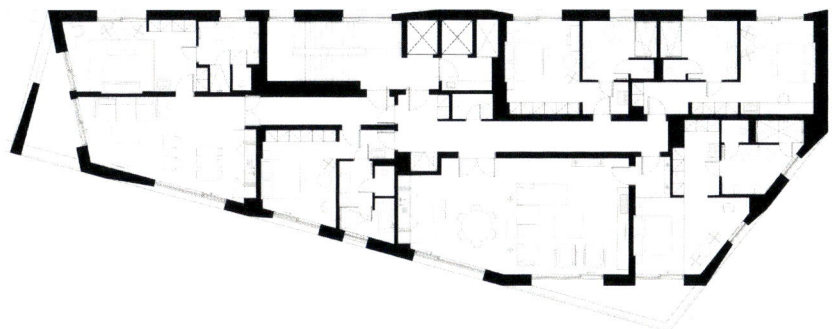

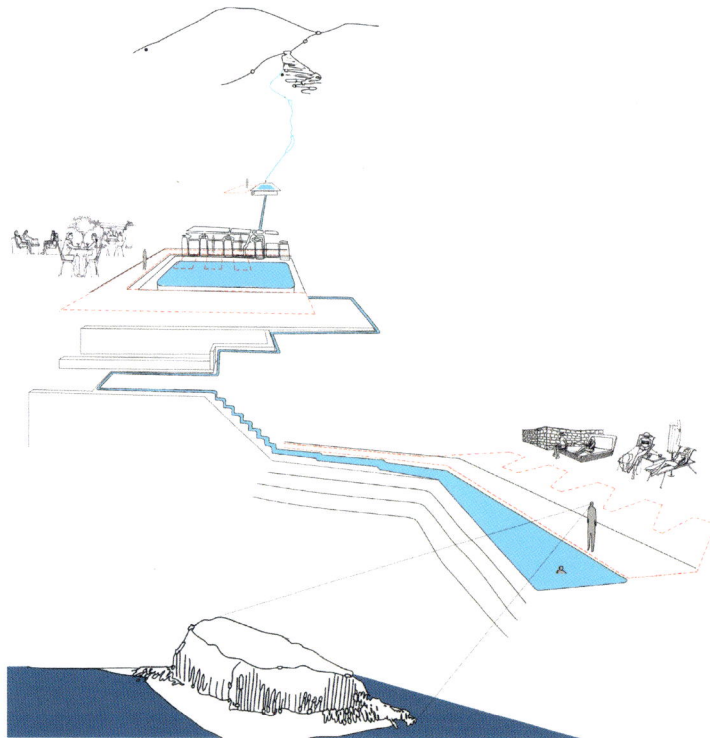

Kinsterna Hotel

—▼—

Kinsterna Hotel is a five-star hotel in the Peloponnese, near the Byzantine fortress of Monemvasia. Surrounded by olive and citrus groves, the 17th century estate has a fascinating past, spanning Byzantine, Ottoman and Venetian times. Revealing these layers of history was integral to the mansion's restoration and conversion into a country hotel and spa. Recreating a self-sufficient and sustainable community was an essential part of our mission to revive this long-abandoned landmark.

Kinsterna, cistern in Greek, is named after the water feature at the heart of the property. For centuries, water has breathed life into this fertile landscape from a source high in the mountains, cascading down a creek before it is channelled into the cistern. Water is the central element of the design concept, weaving nature into the architecture and threading the historic and new buildings together. Irrigating the surrounding orchards, vineyards, and kitchen gardens, water also supports the hotel's environmental philosophy, enabling the revival of traditional activities that were once the lifeblood of the estate, such as wine and olive oil production.

Award

The European Hotel Design Awards,
Shortlisted, 2010

The successive phases of construction are
rendered visible in contrasting stonework
and thick plaster facing.

Divercity Architects

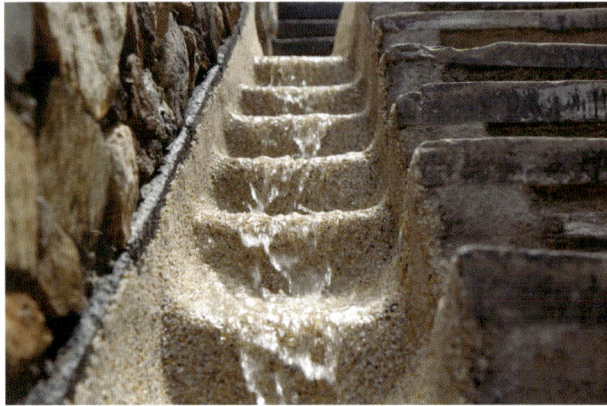

Clockwise from above: Memory is embedded in the textured surfaces of the buildings.

The swimming pool meanders through the grounds like a river.

The main pool is positioned at an angle, extending the views of Mount Taygetus and medieval Monemvasia.

The outdoor dining area, a series of raised platforms floating above the original cistern.

The natural flow of water spills gently into the cistern and pool.

In phase two, we were commissioned to design a substantial extension to accommodate additional common areas. Designing a modern building alongside a historic mansion, while remaining sensitive to the natural environment, posed a number of challenges. Our solution was inspired by the tiled, pitched roofs of Byzantine Monemvasia. We unfolded and extended this recognisable form to create an abstracted roofscape that speaks to the region's undulating hills, as well as the guest's unfurling journey through the estate. Thanks to careful consideration of the position and geometry of the new building, its large volume almost disappears when viewed from the pool. ◄

Clockwise from above: Local construction methods and materials capture the atmosphere of the original building. Ceilings feature exposed stone vaults, cypress beams or traditional woodwork.

Local lace patterns are etched onto the walls, an intimate touch that reinterprets tradition and craftsmanship.

Period pieces are juxtaposed with contemporary design in the suites and rooms.

Skilled local craftsmen were brought in to restore original features like this fireplace.

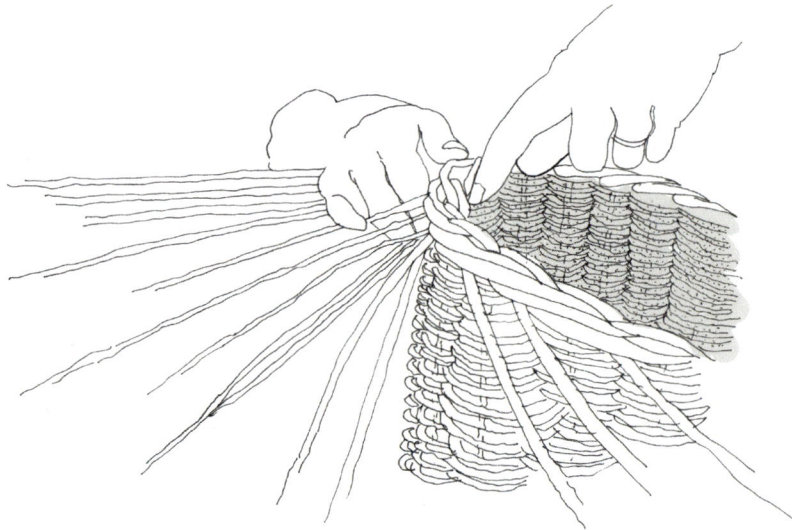

Hytra

—▼—

Hytra is a Michelin-starred restaurant on the sixth floor of the Onassis Cultural Centre, a cutting-edge space for contemporary arts in downtown Athens. To appeal to the young, culture-hungry audience, a new bar and bistro was recently introduced, with a simpler menu offering a modern update on classic Greek dishes. The brief called for a vibrant gathering place that feels welcoming to everyone.

Hytra's emphasis on fresh, locally sourced ingredients led us to reimagine the central bar as a wicker basket, traditionally used by Greek farmers during harvest. Woven from willow branches, the bar doubles as a dining counter, bringing people together to share food and ideas.

The restaurant comes to life after dark when performances take place. To emphasise the theatrical ambience, the wicker bar is back-lit, casting the room in a cosy glow. This subtle lighting effect echoes the building's facade: a white shell encased in bands of white marble. At night, the illuminated building is revealed through the gaps. Like Hytra's tagline, 'bringing new ideas to the table', the space encourages social interaction and creative experimentation.

Divercity Architects

Spetses Summerhouse

—▼—

This striking summer house on the Greek island of Spetses was originally designed by an Austrian architect in the 1970s. Minimal and bohemian, the layout was completely open-plan apart from the bedrooms. The owners invited us to extend, upgrade, and reconfigure the house, defining new living spaces and adding a swimming pool and pool house. We decided to celebrate the vintage aesthetic while bringing the house up to date.

The low-rise, open-plan residence didn't even have a front door. Embracing this sense of wide open space, we added a lattice doorway and canopies that reiterate the exposed stone walls. Painted vivid white, the rough stone walls are a textured canvas for light and shadow throughout the day. Cut-out screens are also used to differentiate spaces and filter the intense sunlight inside the house.

Two is Company, an interior design studio based in Athens, created a full range of custom furniture for the residence. Combining mid-century influences and classical elements, the result is a home with a retro vibe that stays true to its Greek island setting. Since life here is lived outdoors, we added expansive pool terraces and oriented the outdoor furniture towards the views.◀

Clockwise from above: Exposed stone walls and minimal furniture in the light-filled dining area.

Overhead panels with cutaway motifs provide shade and privacy, without creating weight or heaviness.

Surrounded by palm trees, the sleek pool terrace is evocative of a David Hockney painting.

Bespoke furniture in a luminous palette creates a sense of unity and serenity.

Divercity Architects

Libra Head Office

▼

The Libra Group is a global conglomerate that is active in 35 countries. It is focused on six core sectors: aviation, energy, hospitality, real estate, shipping, and diversified investments. Our design for their head office in London reflects the diverse nature of Libra's business. An entire wall in the reception is covered with an abstracted mural of a world map divided across time zones. We collaborated with London-based artists Based Upon to create this one-off metal artwork, which instantly creates a subtle but striking impression.

The extraordinary level of detail and craftsmanship sets this apart from a standard corporate headquarters. Rich, polished wood is offset by pale carpets and muted lighting. Refined materials and a monochrome palette with minimal adornment exude a mood that is understated but uplifting. The overall effect is of a business where quality, attention to detail, and an innate sense of hospitality are paramount.

Clockwise: The high-gloss walnut table
in the boardroom is a bespoke design.

Tactile textures and contrasting materials
in the reception transcend office stereotypes.

Situated in a period townhouse, the offices
are deliberately designed to feel more like
a residential space than a corporate office.

Wood panelling with brass inlays add
a discreet touch of luxury.

The tranquil, informal atmosphere underlines
the fact that Libra is a family business, where
personal relationships are deeply valued.

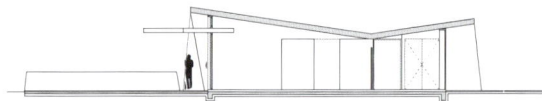

Privacy and enclosure

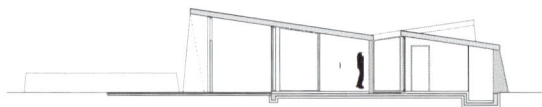

Open living and expansion

Interlocking space

Grace La Dolfina

—▼—

This collection of 32 villas and apartments in Argentina is part of a new hotel and residential complex being developed by Grace Hotels and Adolfo Cambiaso, the world's number one polo player. La Dolfina Grace will be located alongside the exclusive La Dolfina Polo Club, a stunning 465-hectare estate south of Buenos Aires.

Since the performance of the horse is as important as the skill of the polo player, we looked to the equestrian world for inspiration. We found it in the work of the 19th century photographer Eadweard Muybridge, the forefather of motion pictures. Muybridge used a stop-motion technique to demonstrate for the first time that a galloping horse momentarily lifts all four legs off the ground.

The architecture of the villas embodies this dynamic sequence of motion. The contraction and expansion of a galloping horse is expressed in concrete butterfly roofs that seem to float above the vast Argentine pampas. Red brick walls, raw concrete and timber cladding allude to the traditional architecture of local ranches, farms, and stables, reinforcing the strong sense of place.

Divercity Architects

Clockwise from above: The raised roof at the front of each villa blurs the boundaries between indoor and outdoor living.

Bedrooms are tucked beneath the lower section of roof, creating a more intimate atmosphere.

To maximise the hotelier's return on investment, the villas are designed for flexible use: either as private, two-bedroom villas or divided into two separate hotel rooms.

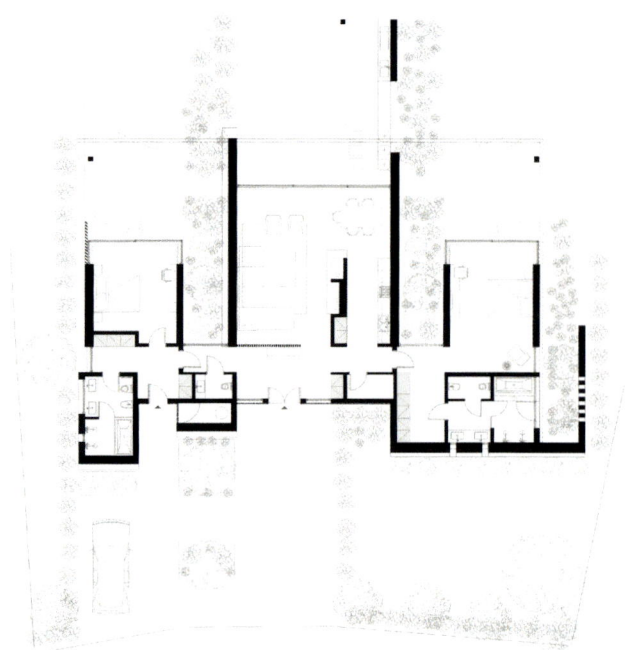

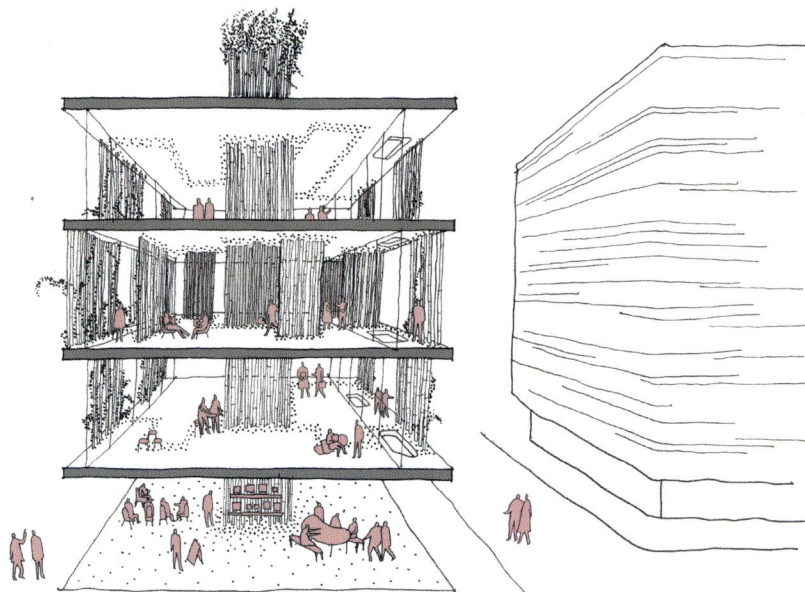

Divercity Architects

Onassis Cultural Centre Office Building

—▼—

The Onassis Cultural Centre is one of the most dynamic arts spaces in Athens. Its aim is to make contemporary culture accessible to everyone. Our redesign of the organisation's head office (the prize-wining design in an architectural competition by invitation) is an expression of this openness. Tectonic architecture, which reveals all the elements of a building's construction, is a clear metaphor for an organisation dedicated to artistic collaboration and creative expression.

We stripped the building facade back to its basic elements; slabs and posts. This strict geometry is softened by the addition of a 'forest' of bamboo poles, placed at irregular intervals to provide moments of shelter or privacy. The spaces in between open up the building to the city, reflecting the organisation's vitality and transparency. Plants growing up the facade suggest a place where ideas can flourish organically. As the plants grow, the building's appearance will change, just like the wealth of ideas within. This linear vertical garden also serves as a visual counterpoint for the Onassis Cultural Centre across the street, which is encased in a horizontal grid of marble slats. More informal, our building is like a dress rehearsal for the main event.

Clockwise: Gaps in the facade increase
interaction between people working
on different floors.

Plants fill the atrium and run up the
staircases, an organic element that reflects
the organisation's sustainable ethos.

Welcoming and playful, the building
reflects the Onassis Cultural Centre's
mission to enrich the cultural life of Athens.

Bamboo poles run through the core
of the building, acting as room dividers
in the open-plan interiors.

Divercity Architects

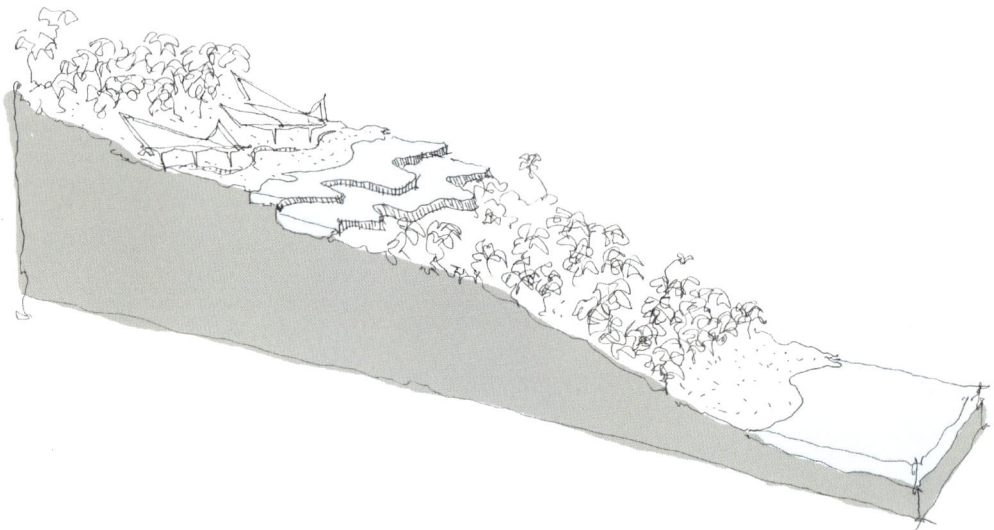

Thailand Resort

—▼—

This five-star resort on the island of Koh Samui is poised on a hillside with panoramic views over tropical forests and out to sea. All 70 bungalows are arranged in rows along the contours of the hills, so that each one has unbroken views.

The rocky coastline below the site is beautiful, but not ideal for swimming. Since everyone goes to Thailand's islands to relax at the beach, we overcame this drawback by creating an artificial beach up in the hills. Working with a specialist company that can build crystal clear lagoons in any location, we created a series of cascading pools surrounded by sandy 'bays'. Terraced pools tumbling down the hillside create distinct settings for different moods, from buzzy beach bars to private coves.

This unique concept allows guests to enjoy the best of both worlds: an exclusive beach resort cocooned in the cool, peaceful mountains.

Clockwise from above: The restaurant's elevated position takes advantage of the commanding views.

Every bungalow features a private pool. Indoor and outdoor areas flow together seamlessly, creating the illusion of even more space for guests to enjoy.

The hotel covers an entire hill, with footpaths through the jungle leading down to the shore.

The bungalows' folded roofs are inspired by traditional Thai sailboats.

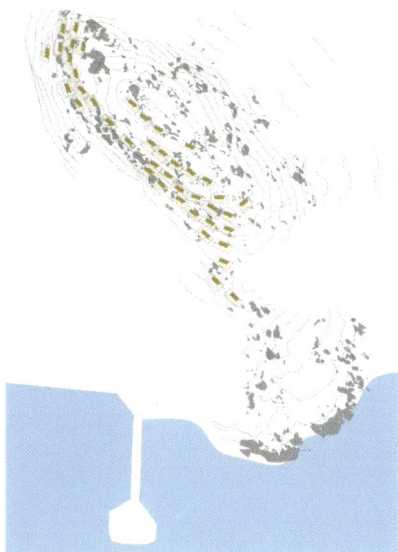

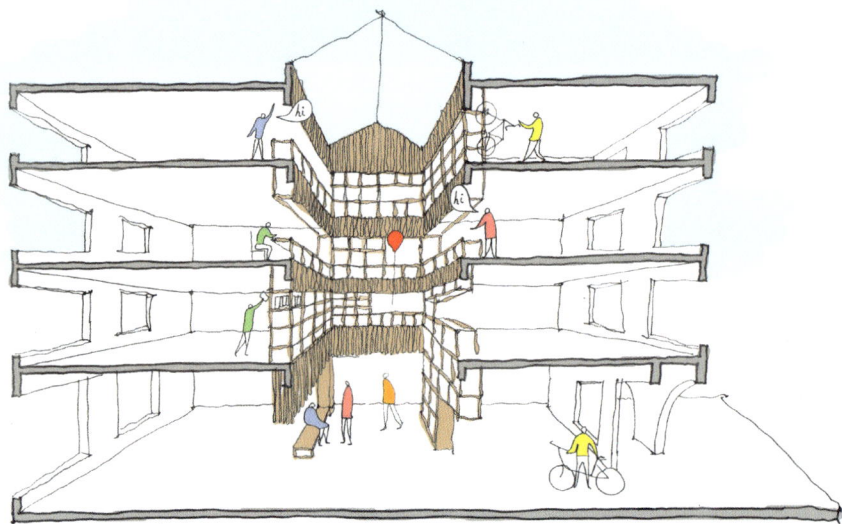

Patras Student Housing

—▼—

This student housing project is located in the repurposed headquarters of The Greek Telecommunications Company (OTE) in Patras, a major port city with a sizeable student population. Built in 1953, long before mobile phones and even landlines were ubiquitous, it was a vital communications hub and meeting place for locals. Our design for this 50-key student residence transforms the building into a vibrant focal point for the younger generation.

While the external frame was preserved, the core of the building was hollowed out to create a three-storey atrium that can be reconfigured in multiple ways. This layout, with rooms radiating around an internal courtyard, is typical of Greek townhouses and well-suited to communal student life. The ground floor is surrounded by a covered walkway reminiscent of Patras' characteristic arcades, a welcoming transition between the halls of residence and the dense urban grid. A new roof garden provides extra space for studying, socialising, outdoor screenings and workshops.

Divercity Architects

Clockwise from above: Flexible and functional, the wooden structure at the heart of the building is a multi-purpose backdrop for study areas, pop-ups, exhibitions and workshops.

To carve out distinct spaces in small studios, beds are placed in cosy boxes with storage built into the walls.

Wooden pavilions on each floor combine practical needs and opportunities for social interaction.

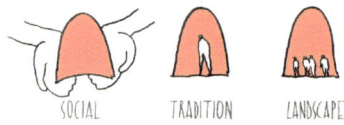

SOCIAL   TRADITION   LANDSCAPE

W Algarve

—▼—

W Hotels are known for their iconic architecture and surprising, sensory environments. Each hotel is uniquely inspired by its destination, mixing cutting-edge design with local influences. With 134 guest rooms and suites and 81 residences, this five-star W resort on the Algarve coast is tipped to be Portugal's new 'it' destination.

We worked closely with landscape designers Scape and interior designers AB Concept to develop a strong narrative theme and eye-catching aesthetics for the resort. Exploring the local landscape, culture, and cuisine, we identified the arch as a common thread, evident in the Algarve's sea caves, the arcades and archways of traditional Portuguese architecture, and the fish scales in the fishing communities along this dramatic coastline. To establish a consistent and dynamic spatial language, we carved out arches of different scales, from the undulating entrance to airy canopies, secret alcoves, and waves of iridescent tiles, inspired by typical azulejo facades. Curved shapes and fluid geometries establish a flow of movement throughout the site, while reflected light adds to the element of surprise.

The curvilinear entrance is an undulating
canopy that provides shade and drama.

Clockwise: We developed a clear visual narrative to unify the large and complex site.

Waves of perforated, reinforced concrete screen bedrooms from the public spaces.

The weather-resistant filter improves ventilation and privacy, as well as creating visual interest.

The facade is clad in iridescent tiles that resemble fish scales.

The arch motif is carried through to the balconies, framing the views of the tiered pools and pine-fringed coastline.

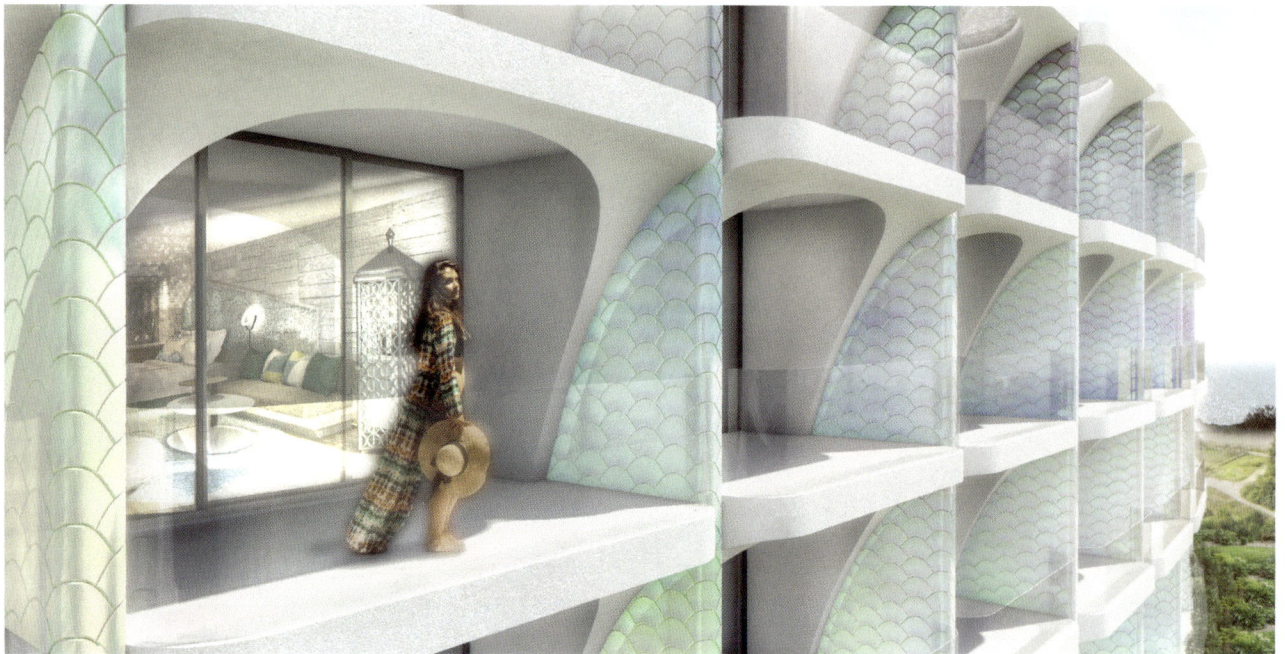

Building D

Building C

Building A

Building B

The wet deck canopy has a radial pattern,
with arched openings on all sides, inviting
guests coming from all directions to
congregate around the bar.

Divercity Architects

Psychiko House

— ▼ —

This residence in Psychiko, a leafy suburb of Athens, had to accommodate several functions: a peaceful family sanctuary, flexible spaces to entertain guests, and a gallery for the owner's significant collection of classic cars and contemporary art.

The house is conceived as a series of surprises. Playing with volume and scale, the architecture juxtaposes curves and sharp angles. Carved out of the perimeter walls, narrow stairways of pale marble gradually reveal different levels and perspectives. The overlapping structure is divided into three distinct zones: a stone-clad core inspired by the fortified Acropolis, an upper floor shaped like a boomerang to frame the sweeping views, and transparent communal areas that occupy the ground floor. A swimming pool ripples alongside the glass-walled living areas, mirroring the fluidity of the spaces within. Mixed materials and sculptural forms create the impression of an ever-changing art exhibition.

Award

The European Union Prize for Contemporary Architecture, Mies van der Rohe Award
Nominated, 2013

Divercity Architects

Divercity Architects

R ough boundary walls offset the reflective surfaces of the smooth, white interiors. The dynamic interplay between public and private space follows through in the upper level, where bedrooms are positioned at angles to take advantage of different vantage points. The effect is like standing on the edge of a diving board ready to plunge into the city.◄

Clockwise from above: The design exploits the tension between opaqueness and transparency, intimacy and openness.

The garage is a gleaming white marble cube containing classic cars and world-class art.

Wedged between stark walls, the narrow entry serves as a passage into a rarefied private universe.

Glazed partitions and skylights allow natural light to flood the interiors.

The curved pool threads alongside the glass-walled living spaces.

Previous page: Jutting above the opaque perimeter walls, the transparent upper floor is imagined as an observatory hovering above the city.

Credits

NIKOLAS TRAVASAROS
Founding Partner & Director, RIBA, ARB
London
&
Founding Partner
Athens

DIMITRIS TRAVASAROS
Partner & Director
Athens

CHRISTINA ACHTYPI
Director, RIBA, ARB
London

DANIEL SILVA
Associate Director, ARB
London

LONDON
Unit 12 Printing House Yard
15 Hackney Road
London E2 7PR
+44 (0) 207 729 5035

ATHENS
Ploutarchou 30
106 76 Athens
+30 210 33 87 563

divercityarchitects.com
info@divercityarchitects.com

ISBN 978-1-5272-366-3-9

9 781527 236639 >